HOME SERIES
DESIGNER BATHROOMS

BETA·PLUS

CONTENTS

P. 4-5
This bathroom was realised by Instore. The bath and washbasins by Boffi (Ifiumi model) and taps by Minimal, also signed Boffi.

P. 6
This bathroom was created by the architect Olivier Dwek. Floor covering in Pebble Stone of Carrara, the back wall covered in handmade Italian grey Opus Romanum mosaics. Wash unit realised by Vincent Van Duysen for Obumex.

INTRODUCTION

Innovating materials, avant-garde forms, new technologies, the range available for bathrooms has changed over the last few years from limited decorative possibilities to a plethora of choice.
Concrete, tadelakt, resin, glass, a new generation of tiles have replaced the perpetual enamel tiles. The bathrooms designed today are highly aesthetic.
Some increasing needs have been added to its main function – often a restricted room devoted to hygiene. Increasing sophisticated and luxurious, over the years the bathroom has become a place for relaxation, a refuge dedicated to wellbeing.
Forget about standard washbasins, today design for personal and original bathrooms meets each person's requirements. Playing the design card at the base, designers and industrials rival each other in creativity and give free rein to all the daring colours, forms and materials. The range has become accessible: even large warehouse names offer ranges of design equipment and accessories at reasonable prices.
True collections offer a specific décor: Zen, exotic, design, minimalist and others to create an ambiance from A to Z. From the bath to the tiniest detail, each universe is defined and conveyed through the design and the materials of these objects.
Having become a main room, the budget allotted to it has increased by 30% over the last decade. A sign of the times, the trend is for contemporary, avant-garde design bathrooms.
This work presents modern, sophisticated, elegant bathrooms with contemporary lines, all examples of enlightened aestheticism.

P. 8
A realisation by
Olivier Dwek.

P. 10-11
In this project,
designed by
Nik Mogensen, small
beaten Marron
Emerador mosaic tiles
were combined with
Buxy oatmeal natural
stone custom-made.
Works in natural
stone:
Van den Weghe
(The Stonecompany).

A MAGICAL AMBIANCE

This spectacular bathroom is located on the top floor of a building from 1911 in the centre of Milan.

Romeo Sozzi, the creator and owner of the top of the range furniture brand Promemoria, dedicated almost two years to the realisation of this project.

The dominant colour is a sombre unusual shade, almost hazel, that gives the whole an intimate and warm atmosphere.

Particular care was taken in the choice of materials: velvet, silk, leather, ebony are ingeniously integrated in projects by Sozzi and contribute to the magical ambiance that reigns in this apartment. Result: an ultra-stylish bathroom and great luxury with timeless elegance. Every detail is important, in a spirit of classic reinterpretation with modern equipment.

A Gong bathroom table in matt nickel and a mirror with a gold leaf frame over the bath.

Shower curtain with buttonholes and rings in matt nickel.

A mirror in matt nickel above the washbasin block covered in lin. Rosa light with a parchment finish lampshade.

Remember...

> The large mirror over the bath, like a visual escape.

> Neon lights integrated in the cornices to diffuse a soft and homogenous light.

> The total absence of tiling, but panelling for a bathroom-sitting room.

P. 16-17
Mirror in matt nickel and Rosa lights. A dressing table covered in leather and bronze towel holder.

URBAN CHIC BATHROOMS

The Upptown team, a visionary property group in Brussels, took on the interior design and consequently also the bathrooms for this exceptional loft.

Three highly typical and stylish bathrooms were designed with high demands for the finish.

Strict lines, simplicity, uniformity are the keywords for these contemporary bathrooms developed as highly structured spaces.

Here the bathrooms are designed in their most essential expression, an almost monochrome minimalism dressed in geometric lines.

A highly pronounced urban ambiance, with harmonies of white and soft green for one bathroom and a white and black contrast for the two others.

Remember...

> The soberness of the lines combined with the glossy black or varnished walls. This strong contrast highlights the design of the baths and gives a touch of sophistication.

SOBER AND PURE

The sumptuous façade of a neo-classical building from the early XVIIIth century houses a superb apartment, recently restored by the architect Olivier Dwek in cooperation with the interior decorator Robert De Groeve.

This bathroom is characteristic of the ambiance that dominates in this apartment: a tasteful blend of pure forms combined with a masterful use of the volumes.

The bathroom of the owners is covered in natural grey Blue Stone Anticato. The 160 cm long washbasin has been integrated in the 350 cm long block realised by Olivier Dwek. The bathrooms were realised by Lapidis.

Décor ideas

> The mirror just above the tiling is totally integrated for a pure design.

> The niche for practical and aesthetic storage.

> The taps on the sink are positioned at the side to prevent it from encroaching on the wall mirror.

AN OASIS OF PEACE AND SERENITY

N oor Zayan, an oasis of peace and serenity, is integrated in the green verdant countryside of Marrakech.

Architect Héléna Marczewsky created a fluid transition there between volumes bathed in light and the outside incorporating patios and large glazed picture windows.

This idyllic space allows you to enjoy an exceptional stay worthy of a thousand and one Arabian nights.

The traditional Moroccan tadelakt techniques were used to give the bathrooms a timeless and warm style.

This bathroom was finished in blue tinted tadelakt. The washbasin table and floor of the shower are in Taza stone.

Floor in grey tinted dusk. The floor of the shower and the washbasin table are made from Taza stone.

Décor idea

> Use tadelakt for a warm and silky effect.
A technique that protects the wall and removes the
use of tiling. It is even used on the floor here.
Good unity nuanced by the different shades chosen.
Bathrooms that invite one to travel and relax.

Bathroom and shower in grey tadelakt. Mirrors by De Bouche
à Oreille.
The horizontal window offers a living tableau at any time over
the domain.

The cupboard in this bathroom was
realised by Kashah. Mirrors by De
Bouche à Oreille. Table in Taza stone.

A ZEN SETTING

This exceptional bathroom was integrated in a loft on two floors situated in a former studio. The space was completely redesigned by the architecture firm Olivier Dwek in partnership with the architect Mathieu De Witte.

They designed a stylish bathroom based on a strong setting.

Accomplished to the tiniest detail, the architecture gives precedence to geometry and balance. The project unveils a bathroom with a mysterious ambiance.

P.26-31
The bathroom-dressing room concept with a freestanding bath.
The tap mouth for the bath was designed by Olivier Dwek. The concrete basin and washbasins were designed by the Dwek firm. The shower is located behind the basins.

Remember...

> The combination and balance between hot and cold materials: tadelakt, wood and glass confront and respond to each other to create a unique atmosphere.

> The perfect symmetry between the bathtub and the two washbasins.

> A well thought through setting: the bathtub sits enthroned in the centre of the room like a sculpture.

LUXURY MIXED WITH SOBERNESS

T he bathroom in this restructu-red and rethought loft by the interior architect Anne Derasse is characterised by a luxurious ambiance, thanks to the materials used but also sober, thanks to the palette of neutral and monochrome colours that make it.

The combination of form and function was scrupulously respected in this project.

The main bathroom with a washbasin unit with pedestal and top from lava stone.
Lighting for the dressing table is completed by LEDs. At the back, the waxed oak dressing table connects to the master bedroom.

The large central shower under a well of light. Taps by Dornbracht.
To the left of the shower, a low bench with storage.

The bathroom dressing table with leather-covered panels dressing at the invisible handles.

Décor ideas

> To keep a comfortable width and corridor, the furniture under the washbasin are narrower than the unit.

> Natural light inundates the large shower thanks to circular wells situated above and calibrated precisely in relation to the size of the shower.

> The complete transparency of the shower positioned here as a central element, the true spine of the room.

P.34-35
The bathroom is treated as an en suite with the bedroom and dressing room. Shaded tones from blue grey and grey green to combine with the lavastone.

VIEW OF THE THAMES

With a magnificent view over the Thames, this superb penthouse on the eighteenth floor of a building in London's Docklands was entrusted to CarterTyberghein. His interior was designed as a unique and highly personalised ensemble.

The bathroom was realised with a real concern for aesthetics: top of the range materials and a well-considered layout. A luxury but unostentatious bathroom.

This bathroom is decorated with Thassos marble.

Statuario marble and dark wood furniture with decorative silver handles.
Round mirror with a white varnished frame.

Décor ideas

> The built-in rectangular mirror above the bath lightens the solid and classical marble wall and gives the visual impression of space.

> The round mirror emphasised in a circle appears to levitate.

The contrast of dark wood and clear marble creates a dramatic effect in the bathroom.

THE SOPHISTICATION

OF EXCLUSIVE STONE

T his bathroom in a vast pent-house was designed and real-ised by the firm of interior architects Devaere.

Here, sophistication rhymes with simplicity. The lines are pure and geometric but with precious covering: natural stone. A perfect balance to create a timeless ambiance.

Unity and minimalism characterise this space where grey and white dominate. A combination that prefigures high ideas of purity.

Individual washbasins and covering of the bath in Grey Tuscan natural stone.

Remember

> The ingenious layout of the basin unit back to back with the bath.

> The turning mirrors on feet allow space to be freed up and the light to circulate.

A WARM AND TIMELESS UNIVERSE

The interior architecture firm Daskal-Laperre realised the complete transformation of a villa for a family with young children.

Functionality, uniformity and simplicity of lines reign in these projects.

One of the bathrooms presents a monochrome ambiance and immaculate white propitious for the restfulness of the mind. The other bathroom is entirely covered in one and the same material, even used for the washbasin. An exclusivity that created a space that is simultaneously pure and practical.

The guest bathroom, installed on the third floor under the roof, is covered in white Carrara marble.

The children's bathroom is realised in green water mosaic with a large bathing area and a separate shower.

Remember

> The partition wall between the bath and the basin unit makes it possible to create a shower at the same time.

> An optical illusion, the vanity cupboard almost disappears thanks to the mirror covering its side.

PURE AND WHITE

The layout of this 200 m^2 apartment was entrusted to the consulting firm Ensemble & Associés.

The keywords here are openness, transparency, soberness, purity, ... The white bathroom offers an ultra-profiled look.

A minimalist décor coupled with the – sparing – use of durable and warm materials like oak cupboards.

Pure and white, for this bathroom in reconstituted stone. The washbasin unit extends into the shower by crossing the glass wall between the bath and the shower.

The oak dressing room in blanched sanded oak leads to the bathroom.

The panelling of the host's lavatory is also in blanched sanded oak.

The guest bathroom. Mosaics in caramel pâte-de-verre and washbasin unit in glossy varnish.

Décor ideas

> The mosaic laid on the walls and floor for a beautiful homogeneity of materials.

> The under furniture lighting: a soft and diffuse lighting that emphasises the covering.

WARM HARMONY

OF COLOURS

T he firm of architects Schellen realised an extremely pure and sober contemporary home.

In any case, a modern but warm ambiance reigns in the bathroom.

Wengé, beige and brown warm up the atmosphere. The reflections of the mosaic also give a soft and refined touch. The décor is not frozen, the vibrant light on this covering contributes to creating a changing surface.

A warm harmony of colours can be found in the parents' bathroom resulting from the combination of the sombre shade of the oak front of the suspended cupboard that holds the washbasin on the one hand, and the dark brown of the glass mosaic that creates the frame for the bath on the other.

Remember

> A chic bathroom thanks to the selection of a range of elegant colours: brown, beige.

> The mosaic around the bath and on the shower wall give brilliance and sophistication and contrasts with the flatness of the brown wall.

> The bath is detached from the coloured wall. A technique that highlights it.

The shower is protected by a large transparent glass door.

SYMPHONY

OF WHITES AND BEIGES

T he firm of architects, Hans Verstuyft designed a contemporary residence with a sober and basic character.

The bathroom presented here is bathed in light. A luminosity accentuated by the whiteness of the rooms. The bath is wisely placed in front of the window to make it possible to enjoy the view while bathing, a true luxury. To shield oneself from any indiscrete viewers, a blind beautifully filters the outside light. This original layout confirms the character of this space and highlights the magnificent bath.

The washbasin unit and the bath were covered in natural stone in sand shades.

BLACK DESIGN

A relatively classical and banal residence was transformed by the architect Pascal Van der Kelen.

A design and minimalist space to evoke purity and hygiene.

This maximal soberness is exalted by the rectilinear forms, the contrasting black and white colours and the avant-garde nature of the materials used.

The bathroom was entirely custom made according to plans by Pascal Van der Kelen. The floor is made from polyurethane, the wall and bath are covered in fibrocement plates.
The shower is covered in black ceramic tiles.

Remember

> The resin floor adds an ultra-contemporary note.

> The continuity of colour on the base of the walls and extended on the bath surround.
This unity of colour creates a niche and a space to relax.

MULTICOLOURED JOIE DE VIVRE

 A large apartment in a green setting was designed by the architect Baudouin Courtens.

In contrast to the immaculate whiteness of the rooms, a few touches of bright colours and golden taps produce a strong contrast. The addition of these few poetic notes quickly transforms this apparently minimalist space into an original and personal décor.

A humorous tableau by Laurent Carpentier.

The bathroom is panelled in white marble from which the fuchsia washbasin unit stands out. The white dressing table leaves the limelight to the jewellery creations of the owner.

Décor ideas

> The splashes of colour bring out the whiteness of the rooms.

> An optical effect, the mirrored doors of the cupboards disappear as they are standing against a wall that is also covered with a mirror.

TIMELESS MODERNITY

A 300 m^2 apartment in Geneva, was rethought and redesigned by the interior architects John-Paul Welton and Brigitte Boiron in combining the classical with timeless modernity with great finesse.

Grey, but sensual, the bathrooms display a firm character. Polished concrete gives a dramatic note to the décor.

Here again the homogeneity between the floor and wall covering is given precedence to limit the diversity of materials. The wooden furniture and black-stained doors give a relative warmth to this room.

The floors and walls in this bathroom were realised in polished concrete.
The wenge mirror is a creation by Welton Design.
The taps and vanity unit: Ottore Meloda, collection Aspara, Riquardi model.
A photograph of the comedienne Emilie Boiron is reflected in the mirror.

Remember

> Polished concrete is similar to a tadelakt
effect: patina and shimmering, reflections.
A warm effect, even with a grey finish.

AUDACITY AND HARMONY

A resolutely New England gentleman's club style was transformed by the firm of architects A.R.P.E. (Antoine de Radiguès) and the general contractors Macors. Lionel Jadot realised the decoration of this countryside home dedicated to harmony and audacity.

The two projects presented here are radically different.

One of the bathrooms shows an atypical face. Extremely classical equipment and covering: it is transformed completely by its unusual ceiling.

The teenager's bathroom. Mondrian found a few reviews and corrections for the happiness of the young lady who inhabits these premises.

The same home, but with an entirely different ambiance, extremely masculine, of a bath and shower room.

A TASTE OF PROVENCE DESIGN

n the surroundings of Aix-en-Provence, a historic country house dating from the XVIIIth century was recently profoundly renovated by its current owners, in partnership with Josselin Fleury (Designer's Studio, Aix-en-Provence).

A dialogue of styles for one of the bathrooms is shown here. The present and the past coexist peacefully: under the old beams, design harmoniously integrates as in the rest of the house. The luxury and sophistication offered by the architectural elements of yesteryear go side by side with a room furnished in a purer contemporary style.

The bathroom of the lady of the house with a Boffi bath in the centre.

P.65-66
The children's bathroom has been treated in a resolutely contemporary style, with fresh and vivacious colours.

Remember

> Combine opposites by juxtaposing a design bath on parquet and under an old chandelier hanging from a beamed ceiling.
This combination instantly creates a scene of timeless charm.

> The original layout: the bathroom is not pushed against a wall as in classic bathrooms but put in the centre of the room to give it maximum emphasis.

Another view of the bathroom p. 64.

A NATURAL AND SIMPLE AMBIANCE

A n old farm was profoundly restored by AIDarchitects (G. Van Zundert/ K. Bakermans).

The restoration was intended to respect the authentic character of the building insofar as possible, without resorting to excessive ornamentation: the idea that prevailed is the creation of a serene environment, intended to give shelter to a young and dynamic family and that gives priority to the functionality of the space.

Use of natural materials, combined with a number of contemporary elements, made it possible to create a special ambiance in this bathroom that brims with character.

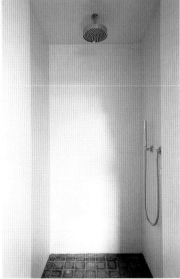

Remember

> The absence of wall tiles makes the bathroom almost a room for living in.

> The glazed door of the shower with a metal frame created a graphic note in the room.

> The wooden bath surround gives greater simplicity and contrasts with the marble top. A combination that echoes the marble basin unit and the wooden shelves.

THE WARMTH OF JURA STONE

T his bathroom from a country-side residence built by Vlas-sak-Verhulst and furnished by Sphere Concepts was covered in Jura stone, a limestone, full of warmth.

The apparent classicism is nuanced through the layout of the equipment and the dominance of white.

The main bathroom. Harmony of painted solid oak, a shower with the sides covered in Jura stone and a built-in solarium.

CONFRONTATION OF ROUGHNESS

AND ELEGANCE

These two bathrooms in a seaside apartment were reviewed by the interior architects from 'aksent. The materials and colours were selected in partnership with Matthijs & co, a general construction company.

As a guiding thread, natural materials, pebbles, wood, slate. Variations on all shades and with the chromatic range of soft colours chosen: from white to fawn.

The children's bathrooms retain a tonal side. The materials were integrated creatively (rough marble mosaic and strips of slate on the floor and walls, rough hewn Douglas pine and edges hand painted on the furniture).
Custom made bronze handles (creation by 'aksent).

Remember

> The diversity of materials in the same space – mosaic, pebbles, slate, tadelakt and wood – gives originality and warmth to the room.

> The numerous spotlights are wisely arranged: positioned above the bath and washbasin, they particularly highlight these elements.

P.74-75
The parents' bathroom was realised in rough "spazzellato" lime wash. Furniture and natural stone are custom made. Leather towel holders (Promemoria).

PARIS DESIGN

n an alleyway of the Parisian "Triangle d'or", that gives out to the hotel Plaza Athénée, the architect and interior decorator Gérard Faivre discovered an apartment of 180 m^2, which he transformed from top to bottom.

His aim was to make the bourgeois values reflected in this very classical property disappear completely, while maintaining the elements that contribute to its authenticity and integrating them into a new highly contemporary ensemble. The result is an ultra design bathroom with a back and forth movement of unconnected skilful elements that create a rhythm.

The bathroom is the best illustration of this highly contemporary spirit.

Décor ideas

> Unusual objects for bathrooms furnish the room. The Bertoia armchair and the statuette personalise the décor.

> Varnished furniture, an increasing trend in precious bathrooms and a touch of the theatrical.

PERFECT SYMMETRY

A t the express request of the principal, architect Pascal Van der Kelen designed a home in perfect symmetry.

Light, geometry and purity characterise this bathroom. A graphic sophistication born from extreme soberness and the strictness of the play on lines.

Positive/negative: the vast varnished black wall structures the space and gives it character by sharply contrasting it to the whiteness and matt finish to the equipment.

The parents' bathroom with walls from enamelled glass and its furniture designed according to the architect's plans.

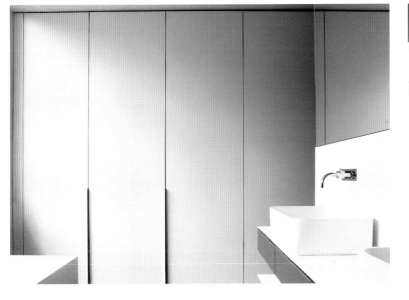

Décor ideas

> A floor in dark resin to create an ultra-contemporary floor.

> The large mirror occupies the entire width of the wall. Positioned in front of the window – without curtains – it reflects outside and multiplies the light tenfold.

SPACE AND LIGHT

F or the renovation of this village home, the customer wanted to give priority to the space and the light.

Daan Van Troyen (architect) and Koen Aerts (interior architect) consequently designed the existing rooms, created additional spaces and a huge annex to the house.

A large level shower with a glazed panel is installed in the children's bathroom. A rough Cotto d'Este stone on the floor. The washbasin unit was also custom made by the interior architects.

Remember

> The immense Italian shower.

> The optimisation of the storage: the high cupboards are discrete because they are covered with mirrors.

The parents' room is equipped with a sober shower room and dressing room.
The shower was custom made in Corian.

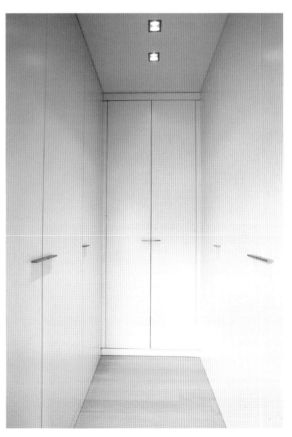

A REFINED APPROACH

D amien Langlois-Meurinne is an interior designer and architect based in Paris. His firm Agence dl-m realised this Parisian apartment.

Result: a top of the range bathroom that reflects a timeless elegance. Select materials, layout, lighting, every detail was carefully studied to design a bathroom outside the norm.

While remaining contemporary, this room emanates a warm and cosy ambiance thanks to the range of colours chosen.

P. 86-89
The bath was covered in Juneda stone. Dornbracht taps. Bronze handles.

Remember

> The perfect symmetry of the layout.

> The spotlights behind the mirrors diffuse atmospheric lighting in a halo.

> The stone only used as base lightens the room.

> Exceptional wooden folding shutters: an aesthetic and original solution that contributes strongly to the décor.

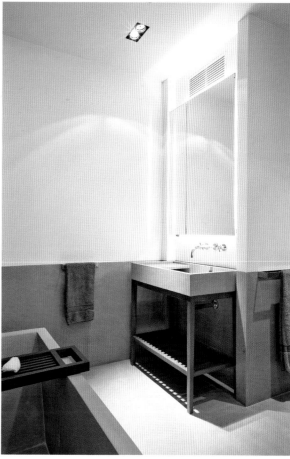

THE BEAUTY OF CALACATTA

Calacatta is a highly exclusive marble, used in this project by the Van den Weghe company (The Stonecompany).

Generally reserved for classical decors, this marble is experiencing a second youth and a transformation as it is nevertheless adapted to furnishings with contemporary and design lines. In doing so, it gives sophistication and magnificence to those premises, which, if deprived of its use would appear minimalist and cold.

The architect Wim Goes created this space full of serenity and timeless beauty.

Remember

> The platform under the bath made it possible to create a so-called "Italian" shower. In addition this elevation magnifies the bath by emphasising it.

ZEBRANO BATHROOMS

L ocated in Saint-Germain-des-Prés in a typical Haussman property, this apartment was restructured by the interior architect Anne Derasse, with a desire for fluidity and purity.

An invitation to travel for this bathroom that one would have thought came from a luxury yacht.

Its strong personality makes one quickly forget its rather limited area.

All the built-in furniture was designed by Anne Derasse.
The bathroom was created through the imbrication of subtly created volumes and concealing a multitude of storage facilities. It is entirely covered in contemporary greyed and stained zebrano panelling. The taps are by Dornbracht.

Décor ideas

> The sombre wood panelling for a luxurious bathroom.

> The contrast between wall-floor with a much lighting type of wood used for the floor.

> The storage areas with a shorter depth house the space under the basin unit and lighten the space.

A LUXURIOUS PENTHOUSE

WITH A VIEW OF THE SEA

One of the numerous bathrooms with a floor level shower. Designed and realised by Obumex.

T he bathrooms in this article are part of a luxurious penthouse on two floors (over 1 000 m^2) with a view of the sea.

All the top of the range finishes: the design and realisation of the ground floor were entrusted to Obumex, which also realised the bathrooms, after a project by the interior architect Philip Simoen.

Décor ideas

> A beach effect for this pebble floor, which creates a relaxing ambiance.

> The sand colour of tadelakt combined with the floor completed this warm décor.

> The vast shower framed by the walls creates a reassuring and intimate space.

Custom-made cupboards realised by D-Intérieur. The bathroom walls are dressed in natural Pietra Piasentina stone. Tara taps by Dornbracht.

A guest room, dressed in Sahco Hesslein fabrics. The custom-made shower and washbasin are covered in Bisazza mosaic. Taps by Dornbracht.

A bathroom in black and silver Bisazza mosaic. Custom realisation by D-Intérieur, according to a plan by Philip Simoen. Tara taps by Dornbracht.

AN INTIMATE NOTE

C ostermans took charge of the interior design of a contemporary apartment building in a serene and discrete spirit.

Given matt and dark walls, the bathroom instantly presents itself as a setting dedicated to wellness. A veritable lazy lounge equipped with a comfortable bench seat.

In this modern bathroom with bronze walls, a clear natural with a uniform colour was chosen. The warmth of the marble mosaic gives a note of intimacy to the shower.

Décor ideas

> The wall light above the bath and the linen blind emphasise the lounge and cosy spirit of this room.

> The recess in the shower makes it possible to sit comfortably in order to relax.

BRIGHT AND COLOURED

his apartment dating from the 1960's has been entirely rethought by the interior designer, architect Olivier Lempereur.

The vast bathroom in this article shows the spirit of this bright and colourful project.

His concept is based on a classical approach: a double basin unit over a large storage cupboard in sycamore wood, suspended 15 cm from the ground for greater lightness. The shower and bath section display a more radical design: stainless steel, glass and immaculate white.

P.100-103
The bathroom with a white Dust Light stone floor and its dressing table in sycamore wood with fuchsia varnish.

AN ATMOSPHERE OF WELLNESS

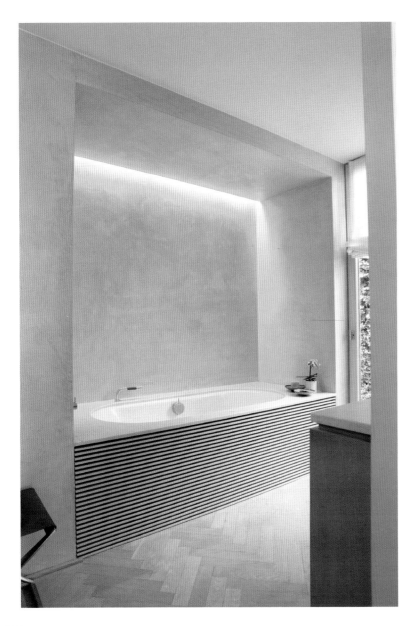

A residence from the 1960's was renovated by the firm AIDar-chitects. The architecture was conceived as a construction game in the rough state, the interior is that of a delicate puzzle that integrates perfectly within it.

Bathed in natural light, a soft ambiance runs through the entire bathroom thanks to the parquet, the use of tadelakt and the wooden furniture.

The play of light and materials creates the image that the bath literally "bathes" in an atmosphere of wellness.

Remember

> The preserved herringbone parquet floor combines with the colours in the room.

> The bath treated like an alcove thanks to the use of tadelakt even on the ceiling.

> A cosy corner accented by the ceiling lighting that diffuses a soft light.

IMMACULATE WHITE

I n this article, the stone company Hullebusch shows a few different realisations in immaculate white.

Purity and design sign this ensemble.

A simplicity and a clear monochrome style counterbalanced by top of the range materials like marble and mosaic.

A washbasin with a Carrare Pocco Veccio marble surface.

Concetto (here the White quartz model) is the top of the range from the Caesarstone collection.

Caesarstone, model 2141, "Snow".

Old white marble mosaic.

A WARM MINIMALISM

These two bathrooms of a 300 m^2 penthouse were realised by the firm of Julie Brion and Tanguy Leclercq.

To guarantee the unity, they mainly relied on varnished wood, natural Italian stone and French oak parquet.

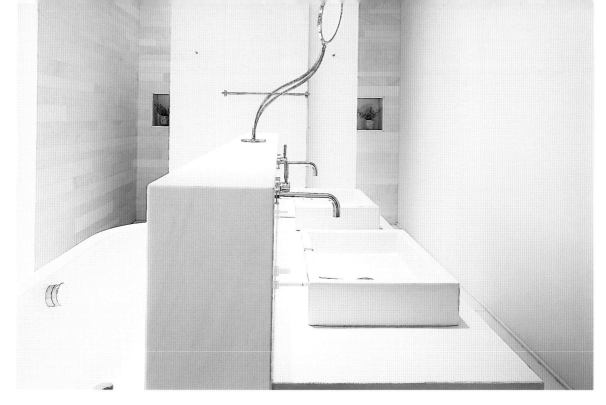

P. 110-113

The master bathroom is exclusively designed using varnished wood and white marble. The look of the wall dressing in linear bands is emphasised by the presence of identical niches in the shower and toilets.

The apparent simplicity of the central island highlights the harmony and technique by which the creators used the varnished wood and white marble.

Remember

> The partition wall holds the basin units and the bath on either side for an original layout. The installation of the water supply and drainage are facilitated in this way and the space is optimised.

Julie Brion and Tanguy Leclercq changed material for the children's bathroom but retained the principle of unity by realising all the elements in stone and the floor in the same Italian stone.

A REMARKABLE

COLLABORATION

The layout of this residential apartment is signed by Filip-Tack design office. He opted for Corton stone for these bathrooms, in close collaboration with the natural stone company Van den Pour Weghe (The Stonecompany). The result, chic and luxurious rooms dressed in a warm colour.

Movable spotlights make it possible to modulate the lighting and to focus on remarkable elements.

The entire bathroom is covered in soft Corton. This white veined stone from Bourgogne was sawn in bands. Solid washbasin and shower floor realised with a suspended system and concealed drainage.

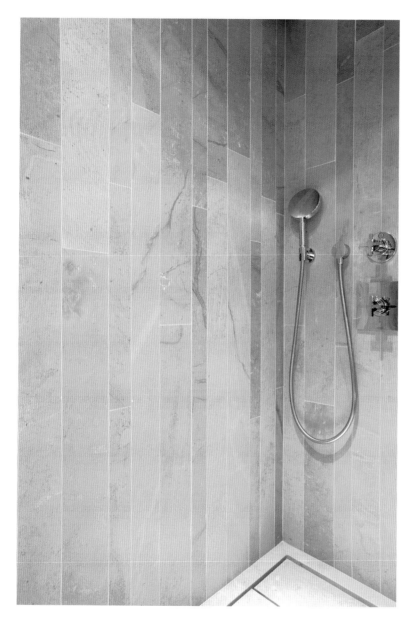

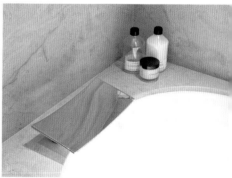

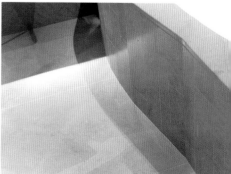

Remember

> A gauge of customisation and originality, the washbasin
unit realised in the same material as the wall covering –
Corton stone – a sign of a top of the range bathroom.

The main bathroom has soft Corton. A double solid washbasin. The shower walls are covered in extra large tiles customer made and with veins running through them. A suspended shower floor.

HOME SERIES

Volume 18 : DESIGNER BATHROOMS

The reports in this book are selected from the Beta-Plus collection of home-design books: www.betaplus.com
They have been compiled in a special series by Le Figaro in French language: Ma Déco

Copyright © 2009 Beta-Plus Publishing / Le Figaro
Originally published in French language

PUBLISHER
Beta-Plus Publishing
Termuninck 3
B – 7850 Enghien
Belgium
www.betaplus.com
info@betaplus.com

TEXT
Alexandra Druesne

PHOTOGRAPHY
Jo Pauwels

DESIGN
Polydem - Nathalie Binart

TRANSLATIONS
Txt-Ibis

ISBN : 978-90-8944-049-5

Printed in China

P.120-121
A realisation by the interior architect
Marc Stellamans in Massangis natural
stone. Panelling in Oregon laminate.

P.122-123
A bathroom in French Sarancolin stone,
combined with Grey Cehegin with a
flame finish.

A realisation by Van den Weghe (The
Stonecompany).

P.124-125
A project by Ensemble & Associés in
Unistone reconstituted stone.
Dornbracht taps and shower head.
Blanched sanded oak furniture.

P.126-127
A realisation by Upptown. Custom-made
furniture in white Corian with a black
glass washbasin.